On War, Whimsy, and The Way

On War, Whimsy, and The Way

Random Thoughts over the Years

JOSEPH PALEN

RESOURCE *Publications* • Eugene, Oregon

ON WAR, WHIMSY, AND THE WAY
Random Thoughts over the Years

Resource Publications
An Imprint of Wipf and Stock Publishers
199 W. 8th Ave., Suite 3
Eugene, OR 97401

www.wipfandstock.com

ISBN 13: 978–1-62032–843-9
Manufactured in the U.S.A.

CONTENTS

PLANE TALK

They said the plane was still on time,
It was 30 minutes late.

Then they said "we're boarding now,"
Another 20 minutes wait.

The plane we're on should be gone,
We still are at the gate.

By now I don't even really believe—
The ". . .bag will not inflate"!

PERSPECTIVE

Billions of billions
Huge blazing balls of fire
Wildly careening at tremendous speed
in all directions.

In a corner of this massive display
A tiny spinning speck of dirt
With brown and green organic matter.

What is the significance of this brown
and green organic matter?
I don't know
But the owner's Son says

He cares about it.

LOVE YOUR ENEMY?

For the fearless
A game of real danger
A skating on ice that is thin

They say you will lose
And you definitely will.
You may not try it again.

But I've heard it said
and I believe it is true;
I've seen it break through the pain.

If they don't take away
your love for them,
you both are the ones
who will win.

ABOUT TIME

Well now I'm retired
I thought not to happen,
But time flows like a river
downhill

I now wash my clothes
and find new time keepers;
The retirement check and
monthly bill

Today I was wondering
as life ticks away
and the dryer clock checks on its fill

How many more dryer loads
left in the account
Before all of the tickers
are still.

THE WOULDN'T BE DISCIPLE

"Sell all you have, give to the poor
Then come and follow me."
A better offer never made
but did not come for free.
To join the band of twelve and heal,
maybe pen a Gospel too,
Was more offer than a diamond mine
but easy to misconstrue.
The guy thought first about his "car,
his boat and hunting gun."
If sold the poor might benefit but
what about his fun?
He did not stop to think it through,
got stuck on the first part.
So left the Lord with only twelve
and a sadness in his heart.

WINNERS AND LOSERS

Who are the winners, the losers today?
they said, as bombs rained down.
I thought we'd learned this lesson well
at least by the last time around.
Well, silly me, whose read history
and should finally dig the scene.
It goes on and on and 'round and 'round
and cold and cruel and mean.
And no one ever wins
not even he who sins by
making all many things that killing so requires.
The profit gained is so soon drained and
the advantage soon expires.
Only God knows why we do not learn and
cease this sickly trend.
And He says one day He'll call it quits and
bring this all to end.
So winner-losers, do not ask;
this game cannot be won.
But if killing must proceed, in the game for the
greed,
Please let me not be the one.

FOR SUPRAPTO
(BELOVED INDONESIAN TEACHER)

We saw a shooting star last night
and have heard the Indians say
the meaning is "a Great Chief has died
and his spirit is on its way."

We later heard that 'Prapto,
our close friend, had passed away.
He was young, and kind, and very smart.
The "why" no one could say.

We sorrow with those who are left behind, and
ask God to sooth their grief.
But now we know the Indians were right.
Suprapto was a Great Chief!

ALL IN ONE?

Three Peoples reaching up to you
Yet among themselves they fight

This cannot be what You want
Please fix it, make it right

Yet it's true that we
We too
Are double minded men

Who love those when they love us back
And ask to be our friend

I cannot see the answer Lord
But killing can't be what's True

Please shelter all the innocents
whether Christian, Muslim, or Jew

WHAT'S IN A NAME

When embryos have to die to
help an old lady regain the use of her brain,
they call it abortion and veto the plan for the Bible's
instructions are plain:
"Thou Shalt Not Kill!"
We agree with that. Still
it seems inconsistent to say:
It is only "collateral damage,"
when little children are blown away!

FINAL EXPENSES

If there's a bill
they must pay
Where there's a will
there's a way

LIGHT AND DARKNESS

There is light
there is dark

There is life
There is death

There is God
There is Satan

If I kill my enemy he comes back
a Hydra, more than before

Someone said I must love him
What a crazy idea

Yet, trying it, a miracle is wrought
He disappears

Vanquished, utterly destroyed
No Hydra heads appear

He has become
a friend

FOR STEVE
AND THE STINGRAY

A stingray is a beautiful fish.
Steve was a beautiful man.
He loved them all, even the snakes,
Tried to help us understand.

He died today, not catching crocs,
nor dodging vicious strikes.
But just swimming there for a children's show
—the end of a guy we liked.

But Steve would say:
"It warn't 'is fault, to kill me was not 'is wish.
Aw came unawares on top of 'im
'e thot aw was a fish."

A PRAYER, WEEPING

Young girls, innocent, trusting; not yet ready to
share
the love inside them.
Must they die to show us where
evil truly resides?
In Iraq?
In our schools?
In our church?
Here, in the hearts of men?
In my own heart?
Help us!
Help us, please, our Father!

A WORLD GONE MAD

I heard them say, "It's a world gone mad,"
and I thought to myself I hope it's a fad—
to do greedy things and not think them bad.
And throw away our joy for big doses of sad.
Maybe, like the disco, it will fade from the scene,
taking with it the greedy and selfish and mean.
And we can again be simple and sane.
But then I don't know—
it's looking like rain.

'TIS THE SEASON

Snow
Icy breeze
Holiday sleaze
Buy, buy, credit-card disease
Garish-weighted-down-over-decorated trees
Sorry
Jesus
Forgive us please

I HEARD THE NEWS TODAY, OH BOY!

Four more soldiers died in vain.
Not enough news to even cry.
So what is all the news about?
Someone poisoned another spy.

ON PUTTING
HUMPTY TOGETHER

How can we say
"We cannot win!"?
When the egg is broken,
it will not spin.

THE SUDDEN LUMP

Did you ever get a real lump
in your throat
when you did not expect to
because it wasn't that sad in
itself but
it reminded
you of something—
like a smell
or a flower
or a sound
or a reading of
my brother's poems.

30000 KIDS KILLED—
NEED MILLSTONES?—
TRY EBAY?

Millstones are not as common as in Jesus' day.
Our methods of milling are new.
But if it is true what the news reports say,
We are going to need quite a few.

For a reference to check Jesus' view on these things
Try Mark, Chapter 9:42

WHAT IS EVIL?

I do not know what evil is,
but I do know more about greed.
I've bought a car I didn't need,
while others starve that I could feed,
and Jesus says to pay them heed,
and I believe in him, yes indeed.

I do not know what evil is,
but, growing in our hearts,
greed is a weed.

SOMETIMES I WONDER

Sometimes I wonder,
(sometimes I cry)
if they won't just try,
instead of lie,
and sell and buy.
And then more die.
Why?

TERMINAL

So what started all this was
I looked up in the night sky and felt
close to God and then thought
It is good to be a child when your father is God.
Then I said
Wait a minute you nut you are not a child and you
are getting closer to God every minute.
Well that reminded me that tonight on TV I heard
a man say,
"The Doctor gave me only 3 to 5 years but maybe
with the right medicine I could in fact last 10" and I
thought
Poor Man!
Oops, do a little arithmetic and I have the same
prognosis.
Wow, an epiphany!
Life is a terminal disease!
Fun though.
It is great to be a child when your father is God!

WHY IS IT?

Why is it that I never see
a spelling error plain as can be,
until later when it jumps out at me?
And fixing these things is never free.
Oh Me!

BLACK HOLE

Modern science is scary.
We hear so many things weird
that shake up our concepts
of how it must be.
And heresy is to be feared.

For example now I understand
that what we see is not real
What seems solid is empty space,
even what we can feel.
The sky is a few percent matter.
Our bodies are empty too.
With the matter part less than one percent.
Hard to believe, but it's true.

But you know I heard back in Sunday School
that God is everywhere.
His Spirit is omnipresent—
inside, outside, here, and there.
Well, I guess He must fill all that empty space and
somehow I feel better now.
When I pray to Him he is right inside—that con-
cept gets a "Wow!"

Black holes, though, I understand, completely have
no space.
Even no light can penetrate—for God there is no
place.
Jesus says, "How deep is the darkness"
when the Light of God we lack.
So if our life has a hole,
we should get it filled,
Before we hear "fade to black."

A TRIBUTE / 2 SAMUEL 6

Uzzah in back, Ahio in front
and on the cart: The Meaning of Life.

Ox stumbles, Uzzah reaches quickly
to protect the precious cargo.

They said God was angry; I mean no disrespect
to say I don't think so.

Rather, He might have said
"Heaven needs you, Uzzah," a man
who knows his duty and leaps to it
without thought of consequences.

ON PLANNING A WAR

I read in the Bible they inquired of God,
before contesting on foreign soil.
To tell them whether they could win,
or if Satan their plan would foil.

We now are confused about this step.
We think winning due our own toil.
So instead of asking permission from God,
We just inquire of Big Oil.

(M)ILITARY (I)NDUSTRIAL (C)OMPLEX

They say be afraid—"WMD!"
Then they say "must fight
so we'll be free."
And watch out for terrorists
behind that tree.
But we know it's not the WMD
or terrorists that hate if we are free.
The real problem here is apparent to me.
Like Ike said before,
It's the MIC.

LONDON BRIDGE

London Bridge is falling down.
Like us, they thought it would.
Another bridge had cracks and twists.
They said: could that be good?
But money's always hard to get
for bridges, roofs or roads.
We must do war and give back tax
to those with many abodes.
The answer is to privatize,
corporate bridges and a toll.
Like olden days, we will pay
under the bridge to a Troll.
The moral of this tale is no morals left,
no one to make it right.
The profit-for-profit-only machine
 sucks from us day and night.
I guess a Messiah is what we need
to free us from those folks,
and take their yokes from off our necks
to place His easier yoke.

ON AND ON—
A WAR GONE LONG

On and on and on and on.
Where have all the soldiers gone?
There is no end if you don't end it,
No saving grace if you don't send it.
The days are breaking but there is no dawn.
On and on and on and on.

DO YOU EVER?

Do you ever wonder
how it might have been
If you had
made
a different choice and
married that other girl
who wanted to but you thought the other one
was cuter?
What a way to guide a life,
Cuter!
Or
Is it all done for us and we really had no choice so
we really are not to blame are we?—
just hang on for the ride of your life—
don't let go!
"Arms and legs in the car please!"
Do you ever wonder?
I do

WAY NOT WAR

Bombarding war news has taken its toll.
It deadens the mind and poisons the soul.
The poison runs in all our streams,
Bomb them again,
We won't hear the screams.
The channel is switched to a happier sound
American Idol, who's winning this round?
And some dogs are lost, children too.
Save the whales and the apes.
What else is new?
Oh yes, we must vote.
Who is handsome and tall,
and most patriotic, to shepherd us all?
For we, like the sheep, have gone astray.
We call for revenge, but say that we pray
For God's will to be done. We better take care—
the bombs we have dropped, the failure to love—
WMD might rain from above.
More war will not end it, but peace can be true.
If we want God's approval we must start anew.
Stop hiding our heads under the sand. Bow them
instead;

Try. Understand
that by loving all others we won't get our way.
It's the Way we must take if we wish to stay
Out of war, out of killing, and hating mankind.
A Way some must know but few ever find.

The narrow path means we give up on some
things—
Our greed, not our Freedom, which the Way gives
real wings.
It does, I admit, sound too good to be true,
A world full of caring, a world truly New.
But we must teach the children that such things
can be
For them if they practice this new kind of FREE.
Others are first; with God for our guide
We walk with, not hate, our brother by our side.
And God will smile and Bring Peace to the land.
At least for our children; on this Hope I stand.

I DON'T KNOW

I don't know what Heaven is,
But I know about Hell on earth.
Because I was there and now I'm free;
Was worthless, but now have rebirth.

I don't know what the Spirit is,
But I know just how it feels
To ask for help and have power flow
Inside, so strong it is real.

I don't know who Jesus is—
Prophet, rebel, or King.
But I do know His words* have
Brought me peace, and of this
Today I sing.

*Matthew 7:7

LET THEM EAT CAKE

"Sir,
The people are desperate; they're losing their homes;
It's awful out there, to be frank."
"Uh,
I am concerned, but don't bother me now;
I'm busy rescuing this Bank!"

THE SECOND CHANCE

Two shattered figurine pieces;
each only half its original
and unable to stand.
Glued together in a fit
so imperfect, yet so necessary.
Getting legs again
and enough balance
to go on.

THE FOX'S CASE—
RE 2008 ELECTION

The Fox said it's a shame and we will not stand for
more.
Someone has been in the chicken coop—we must
close that door.
Perhaps the chickens have attacked themselves, but I
think this awful deed
May have come from some bad foxes; those carried
away by greed.
This maverick Fox is another breed; I will not stand
for such hell.
Put me in charge of the chicken coop and again all
will be well.
Only honest foxes will be in charge, in the plan I
have in mind.
With no more raiding and no more greed—foxes of
a different kind.
So if you think a fox in the coop seems to be insane,
Just put this maverick Fox in there and see if things
don't change.

THE VENEERED ONE

Sure, I'm a Christian, I'm glad you can tell.
So sorry for all those going to Hell—
Those evil names like Ahmad and Hussein—
Who refuse to accept Jesus, those children of Cain.
I believe in Jesus, He has saved my soul.
I lined up and said so when I was 8 years old.
That bum on the corner, I'll bet he has sin,
If I give him a dollar, he'll just go buy gin.
Those people next door they are almost worse.
I know they would never darken the door of a
church.
What's this you say about the "least of these"?
Poverty is a self inflicted disease.
You are poor if you're lazy and no other reason.
Remember the ants and saving up for the season.
I don't have to read what Jesus said.
I accept Him, and that's it! I'm saved from all dread.
And I love my country, God's chosen for sure.
With His help and our courage the flag will endure.
So don't give me all that socialist stuff,
Or say "read the Bible," I know it enough.
It's where all the Verses are kept.
I know the shortest one:
"Jesus Wept."

THE FINANCIAL BLUES
IN BROKE FLAT

The banks are getting billions,
Investment companies, too.
The auto makers stand in line
To also get their due.
I guess we have a lot of dough
The way we throw it around.
I thought they said that "spread the wealth"
Had a socialistic sound.
I don't care what they call it,
But us folks are getting blue.
And if they want us to buy their stuff,
They better give us some too.

HOPE FROM 2009

King came and said
and died.
Jesus too—
The poor, the blind, the black—
Those oppressed without the funds
to make it right—
Or the good old boys to
cover their back.
This guy came now and told us too
to not yet give up hope.
We needed that so much, so much—
so hard in these times to cope.
So pray for him and pray for us and
pray for the days ahead.
So hard and yet,
with love we can
bring change from the ruins and the dread.

THOUGHTS OVER MANY YEARS

oh for the courage
to let go the branch
carried into life's stream
the stream becomes stable, buoying
life flows by instead in a fascinating
unending display

written years ago
when searching desperately
still searching but
no longer lost
having found the door

THE POOR IN SPIRIT

They said God helps those who help themselves.
I tried hard to conform.
The program called for drink and drugs.
Live hard and fast was the norm.

God seemed to not care—he wasn't around.
"There is no God," they said.
So live it up in the here and now.
'Cause when you're dead, you're dead.

But God just laid back and gave me rope.
Enough to hang on it's true.
But when I got to the end of that rope,
there was God there too.

He seemed to say "I help them all,
because I love them, you see.
And surely he who can't help himself,
whenever he turns to Me."

NEWS BLUES

Heerd today from TV man
'conomy 'bout to fold.
So I lissens real caref'ly
to do what I is told.
But don't believe him when he say,
"IT'S EASY TO OWN GOLD"!

AT HALF MAST ON 11–10-09

We stand in rows to honor them
whose lives were taken by another like them
also in uniform but not uniform in purpose.

Fine men and women in uniform
trained with their weapons standing ready to fight
as such brave volunteers, there for country, despera-
tion, or lack of job,
prepare to defend as they did in World War II
when the Enemy also had guns and uniforms and
stood in line.

Our Enemy has no uniform except a uniform hate
burning in desire for revenge
of supposed wrongs and real wrongs done long ago
and yesterday.

How do we shoot this Enemy? How many? Where?
We call them a Name, but
what is in a name? Better we call them Hate. Can
we kill Hate with guns? Can we put out a raging fire
by putting on more fuel?

Our Soldiers, may God bless and protect them,
are not to be blamed—they are to be admired and
deeply respected for the will to serve and the skill
they display.

But we must not continue to send them to fight one
war when the Enemy fights another.

Help us God to see the way—a way to fight Hate.
You said we fight Hate with Love.
But how, Lord, how do we befriend an angry
wounded tiger?

Our certainty and glibness fails us.

We humbly pray.

VALENTINES DAY

I'm thanking you God for the concept of love,
which if we have tried
means we have cried
because of our pride
but it changed us inside
and our selfish self died.
Such pain and peace comes only from above.

REVERSIBLE AND IRREVERSIBLE

A mistake on the computer—press a button to undo.

Some chemical reactions are reversible too.

But words make it hurt when they're over the top
and wars—
These are easier to start than to stop.

THIRD TIME—33 YEARS
AND COUNTING

I tried to live life
just me and her
just her and me
we needed no one else I thought.

But it was not what I expected—
she would not change to meet my needs
I did not change to meet hers.
The void was not filled.
Angry and disappointed,
we divorced in a chorus of blame.

That was even worse, the void, the pain, the need
was too much.

Maybe, we thought, if we try it again it will work.
So we started again from the top of the page
But, repeating, results were the same.
The void not filled was growing deeper; the channel
was not to be bridged,
so divorce again was the only way,
and it hurt even more and we tried to drink it away.

Finally it dawned; the void was special that no hu-
man person could fill
I turn to God and cried "heal me, if it be your will."
Now settled with another, but no repeat.
This time there are not two but three.
With the Spirit of God filling both of our voids,
we are not just one to one
but Him to her and to me.

MIRACLE

It sounds strange,
but Jesus says it's true—
You are not God,
but God lives in you.

THE WAY OF THE WORLD

Forgive us Lord
that we have
Thrown you out for shallow learning,
Instead of
Opening our minds to deeper Truths.

IN THE BEGINNING,
GRAVITY. . .

They have recalculated, and now they can show
Gravity created the Heavens and all below.
God, they say, is not needed now;
"Gravity does it and we can show how"

But God might say "hey wait there a minute;
I created the world and all that is in it.
That includes your math, and also you;
And, by the way, I made Gravity too."

COSMIC THEOLOGY—I

There was not time nor need for it
And the void was filled with black
God showed His might
The Bang was pure light
And the darkness was pushed back
The process went on
The stars were formed
And around them the planets sped.
Then molecules in array
DNA led the way
And life came bursting through the dead.
On and on grew the life, guided by DNA
A programmed plan to create man,
At least that's what some say.
I believe that all this could be true,
And did happen because of a plan.
And someday when we go to another place,
We'll find out why God created man.

INEVITABLE

Resolutely moves the huge barge of state
down the river of time toward
the Falls—fate of all before.
Desperate paddles dip in to try to steer
by both parties equally
ineffective
to turn the boat toward a saving shore
while those always lucky ones ride
unconcerned
knowing their bankroll will get them
to the bank in time.

BALANCING THE BUDGET

Morning, I hear a mighty roar—across the sky—a
machine of war—how much does it cost; what is
lost?—can it reach our goals; protect our souls?—we
close our schools—are we fools?

SUNBREAKS

On the front porch soaking up the vitamin D.
Doctor says.
In Oregon the low winter solstice sun floods the
front porch,
Only this time of year.
On shorter and less reliable cycles the sun peeks from
behind the ubiquitous clouds.
Did I mention it is Oregon?
And wonderful?
Where the sun, once not obstructed, beams through
sky so pure that it almost burns the face
in December.
Wonderful.
And Warm.
This dangerous and frustrating world must have
sunbreaks.
So God provides.
Makes it worthwhile?
Oh Yes!
But now the sun-swallowing clouds move in again,
leaving only a still warm face.
(And a bad prose poem in the head)
A woman walks by
at full speed maybe for the bus to a job.
I silently wish her sunbreaks today at her work.

4 MORE

4 more died today
the Demos are in, I heard them say but
4 more died today
we stopped those right wingers, held them at bay
but
4 more died today
how can we help it, what part can we play
4 more died today
we'll meet and plan, please don't delay
4 more died today
we do hope to change things, what more can say
4 more died today
it is NOW we must we change the game that we
play because
4 more died today
4 more died today
4 MORE DIED DIED DIED DIED TODAY!